NORTH WESTERN
RAILWAY OF INDIA

ALON SITON

AMBERLEY

First published 2023

Amberley Publishing
The Hill, Stroud
Gloucestershire, GL5 4EP

www.amberley-books.com

Copyright © Alon Siton, 2023

The right of Alon Siton to be identified as
the Author of this work has been asserted in
accordance with the Copyrights, Designs and
Patents Act 1988.

ISBN 978 1 3981 1445 6 (print)
ISBN 978 1 3981 1446 3 (ebook)

British Library Cataloguing in Publication Data.
A catalogue record for this book is available from
the British Library.

Origination by Amberley Publishing.
Printed in the UK.

Introduction and Historical Background

Presented with a book about the history of the North Western Railway of India, the reader is rightfully bound to ask 'why specifically that railway?' After all, the NWR was but one of several large railway companies operating in British India. It was fundamentally similar to the Bengal Nagpur Railway, as an example, or the Madras & Southern Mahratta Railway, two other notable Indian railway systems. Essentially, it was all about running scheduled passenger and freight trains in the service of the general public. The NWR, however, was an exception to that rule. Formally a member of British India's giant railway network, the NWR was vital for Britain's geopolitical plans in central Asia. Its strategic importance in the implementation of these plans cannot be overstated in any way. All of British India's railway companies were routinely engaged with the country's domestic concerns, moving passengers and freight in times of peace and troops in times of war. The NWR provided the same type of service, but was additionally required to operate British military trains into what one day would become Pakistan. Reaching deep into the Indian frontier, NWR trains were regularly sent hundreds of miles away from Delhi and Lahore, now on both sides of India's border with Pakistan, to such remote destinations as Quetta and Peshawar. Beyond the border were Kabul, Kandahar and all of Afghanistan, the so-called 'graveyard of empires'. More to the north was Russia, which at the time was Britain's biggest rival in the race for domination in Asia. It was no secret that, long before 1914, the Russians were determined to own a warm water seaport in the south of Asia. Equally important was the discovery of oil in the region. Stuck between two major European powers, Afghanistan was suspicious of any attempts to establish any foreign presence in the country. This was not without a good reason. Britain and Russia were already locked in a race for supremacy in nearby Iran. The competition was fierce enough that war between Britain and Russia would in all probability have broken out, were it not for the signing of the British-Russian convention of 1907. Diplomacy saved the day, but the agreement was reached over Iran's head, prioritising British and Russian interests over Iranian ones. Iran could be likened to a deer feeding two tigers, an accurate metaphor in Brian Lapping's monumental book *End of Empire*: 'thus did the tigers divide up the deer'. In the decades that followed, Afghanistan was invaded by the Soviet Union and the United States, with disastrous consequences for both sides. It is tempting to draw a conclusion about the true cost and wisdom of sending a fully equipped army to fight a war in a country such as Afghanistan. The latest tragedy, following the withdrawal of US forces after twenty years of American military and political involvement in Afghanistan, is a painful reminder that history sometimes can and does repeat itself. This book will therefore also offer an overview of the railways of Pakistan, emphasising their relevance to the NWR.

The story of the North Western Railway of India is in many ways the story of both pre- and post-partition India itself. Strategically crucial for Britain's rule of the Indian subcontinent, in the Partition of India in 1947, the NWR was faced with a whole new challenge when the western half of the system came under new Pakistani control. Resembling the situation in the Middle East, long-established rail and road links were severed overnight due to a new political reality. Worse, the creation of the two new states had escalated the religious hatred in India, leading to an outburst of violence on an unprecedented scale. Millions of people were forced to migrate across the newly drawn borders between India and Pakistan. Around 700,000 refugees travelled by train between 14 August 1947 and 8 September 1947 alone. The uncertainty surrounding the exact boundaries and the helplessness of those who lost their homes and livelihood only aggravated the catastrophe. Desperate to reach any safe place, overcrowded refugee trains were given military escorts to protect their passengers from vicious attacks. On a single day in November 1947, four trains left Jullundur City for Lahore with a total of 16,000 Muslim refugees. Even that wasn't enough to get the refugees out of harm's way. A train carrying some 3,000 refugees started from Bannu on 10 January 1948. The next day that same train was attacked at Gujrat station. Hundreds of refugees were killed and injured. The following years were a time of unrest in Punjab, Kashmir and all along the Indo-Pakistani border. Torn apart by religious, political and ethnic differences, both countries were trapped in a series of wars, leading to more death and suffering. A change for the better, however, may be on the way. The Samjhauta Express is a passenger train connecting New Delhi with Lahore. Translated to 'The Agreement Train', this train is a promising sign of peace in an area hitherto dominated by death and dispute. One can only hope that, when all is said and done, a full and lasting peace between India and its former foe will be achieved.

For their generous help and assistance in the making of this book, I wish to thank Greg Martin, Helmut Dahlhaus, Keith Chester, Mark Carter, Omar Mukhtar, Salman Rashid, Paul Graalman and Alexandre Gilliéron. Special thanks are due to the late Percy Stuart Attwood Berridge, the legendary railway engineer who will forever be associated with the North Western Railway of India.

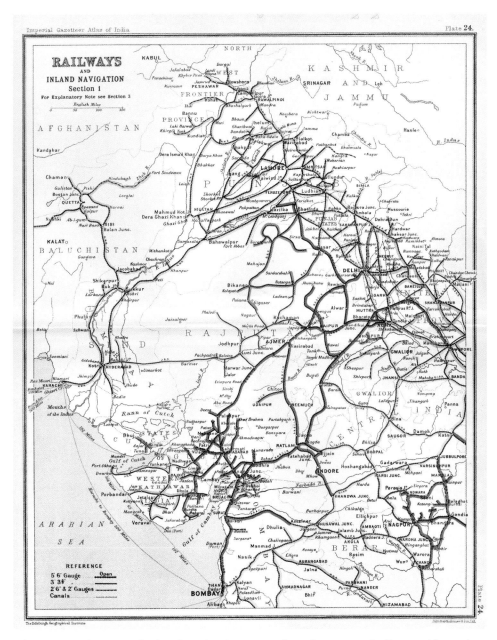

This 1931 railways and inland navigation map of north-western India provides a clear view of the NWR main lines connecting Karachi with Delhi and Peshawar. The bulk of the NWR system was centred in the densely populated Punjab region. More to the west are the frontier lines to Quetta, Chaman and Landi Kotal. The start of the Nushki Extention, leading to Iran, is visible to the left of Quetta.

British India

Much has already been written about Britain's colonial rule of the Indian subcontinent. The historical background which led to the creation of the Indian Empire will therefore be mentioned here briefly to provide the reader with the necessary context.

'In the beginning there was the Bible. Then there was Britain and finally there were the railways' – these few words effectively tell the story of British India and of the entire British Empire. The combination of God, Britain and the railways remains to this day the defining element of the bygone days when Britain ruled the seas and the railways were the lifeline of its many colonies around the world. This was particularly true in the case of India, Britain's biggest territorial possession, which came to be known as the jewel in the crown of the British monarch.

The road to British presence in India was paved as early as 1600. Queen Elizabeth I granted a royal charter to a group of British merchants wishing to explore the riches of southern Asia. Thus was created the East Indian Company (EIC). In 1640, the EIC succeeded in securing a piece of land in southern India, thereby signalling the start of the gradual British penetration into the rest of the country.

British forts and settlements sprang up all around India and the British were now leading traders in precious Indian goods. By 1760, India was rapidly coming under direct British control. Any opposition was crushed by force. When the military campaign ended, the whole of India was subjugated to Britain. The foundations were laid for a new empire that was bigger than anything that the British had ever dreamt of.

By the mid-nineteenth century, Indian nationalism was beginning to take form. There were loud demands for social and economic reforms. These strong sentiments resulted in the Indian Rebellion of 1857, which, although brutally suppressed, also led to the transfer of power from the East Indian Company to the British government. The railways, a tangible symbol of the British influence, had been a target during the rebellion. The British were quick to learn the lesson from the rebellion. It was a catalyst for widespread railway construction, with a view on deploying troops throughout India.

The British Raj in India officially began in 1857. The Raj (literally 'rule' in Sanskrit), also called Crown Rule in British India, included the princely states, which were ruled locally by indigenous princes and maharajas, under British control. The Raj ended in 1947, with the partition of the Indian Empire into two sovereign states – India and Pakistan, whose eastern part later became Bangladesh. The Raj consisted of eight main provinces under a British commissioner or governor, these being Assam, Bengal, Bombay, Burma, Central Provinces, Madras, Punjab and the United Provinces at the foot of the Himalaya Mountains. In 1900 alone, these territories had a combined area that was several times bigger than all of the United Kingdom.

India's railway history is known to have started with a pair of small industrial lines. The first one, in 1832, was the Red Hills Railway, which was part of a road-building project in Madras. The second line was built in 1845 to carry rocks for the construction of a new dam over the Godavari River (India's second longest river). Then in 1845, the East India Railway (EIR) decided to hire the services of experienced railway engineer Frederick Walter Simms. Simms was previously involved in the South Eastern Railway in England. He succeeded in persuading the EIR that a new line from Calcutta in the direction of Delhi would be a suitable venture. Construction of the railway progressed rapidly and the first section of 120 miles from Calcutta was opened in February 1855. Sir Alexander Meadows Rendel was the consulting engineer responsible for the design of its many bridges and other infrastructure. He was also involved in the design of similar structures along the Bolan Pass line, on the other side of the subcontinent.

Also in 1845, the Madras Railway was formally established. In 1849, the Great Indian Peninsula Railway (GIPR) was incorporated. Elsewhere, in eastern India, the first East Indian Railway passenger train left Howrah (near Calcutta, now Kolkata) to Hoogly (West Bengal), a distance of 24 miles, in August 1854. The line carried 100,000 passengers in its first four months and turned out to be such a success that the company decided to extend the railway to Delhi, a distance of 900 miles. The Punjab followed with the Scinde, Punjab & Delhi Railway in 1870. By 1871, India's four major cities – Bombay, Delhi, Calcutta and Madras – were all connected by railway.

The Indian railway system continued to grow right through the turn of the century and the First World War. The Indian Frontier Mail made its inaugural run between Bombay and Peshawar (today in northern Pakistan) in 1928. The Grand Trunk Express began running between Peshawar and Mangalore, and the Punjab Limited served Bombay and Lahore. In 1947, considerable changes were made to the Indian railway system following the end of the British Raj and the Partition of India. Under the new political reality and the division of the subcontinent into several new states, the national system was reorganised into new administrative regions under the Indian Railway Board.

By 1910, the Indian railway system had become one of the largest in the world, with a total of 42,000 miles of multi-gauge track divided among fifty-eight companies. The North Western, East Indian, Great Indian Peninsula and Bengal Nagpur lines, with the main lines of the Madras & Southern Mahratta (MSMR) and the Bombay, Baroda & Central India (BBCIR) Railways, formed the main routes and were all broad gauge. The secondary railway systems of central and southern India, Burma and the state of Assam were mostly metre gauge.

The railways helped to unify India. As well as the vast size of the subcontinent, there was the climate, which changed from the steaming heat of the south to the freezing cold of the Himalayan north. The journey from Bombay to Peshawar, for example, began in tropical heat and ended in the freezing conditions of the North-West Frontier Province. The geographical difficulties varied from high mountains and dry deserts to tropical jungles and malarial swamps.

The 1920s were marked by a steady rise in the number of tourists and visitors travelling to India, along with an improvement in the living standards. One notable aspect of this was the introduction of long-distance mail trains, which became necessary since India's main cities are all hundreds of miles apart. The destinations selected for these corridor trains were Bombay, Madras, Calcutta and Karachi, along with Delhi and the North Western Frontier.

Two famous examples of these important trains were the Bombay-Delhi Frontier Mail, operated jointly by the Bombay, Baroda & Central India and the North Western Railways, and the East Indian Railway's Delhi-bound Punjab Mail. Both trains covered a distance of 900 miles in twenty-three hours, including stops for locomotive changing, platform time and refuelling. The Grand Trunk Express, India's longest direct railway route, departed from India's southern tip at Mangalore and proceeded due north through the cotton-growing flatlands of the Deccan Region to the Punjab and Peshawar, the gateway to the lands beyond the Himalayan mountains. This train covered a distance of 2,497 miles in a little over ninety-six hours.

India received its independence from Britain in 1947, officially ending the colonial period in the subcontinent. The new reality of self-rule was also a turning point for the railways of India, whose giant system was in a condition that was far from perfect as a result of the Second World War and the gradual decline in new investment in infrastructure ever since the 1930s.

Upon the British administration's departure, the railways were arranged not as one single company, but as a patchwork of separate systems lacking any standardisation of rolling stock and equipment. A good many of India's steam locomotives were shipped overseas to help with the British war effort. The ones that remained behind were often cannibalised for spare parts. There were only a few new orders for rolling stock, in part due to the war's impact on the British economy and the difficulty of manufacturing new locomotives. The supply of new equipment for the railways both at home and in the colonies abroad had to wait until production could be resumed, but only after peace was restored in Europe and the British industry was back on its feet after the long war years.

One immediate outcome of India's independence was the carving up of the Raj into several new states, outside the borders of a smaller India. The political lines on the map were redrawn to reflect the desires of the hostile Hindu and Muslim communities that were previously living under one central British rule. The Partition of India was essentially religiously motivated, so that followers of each specific faith were given a piece of the total territory.

For the railways of the former Raj, this created yet another problem. Whole sections of the Indian system were now across the border and out of reach. The railway companies themselves were already transferred from British to Indian hands and, after a transition period, the latter were expected to assume responsibility over the country's national railway system, while taking into account the complicated political relationships with Pakistan, Burma (now Myanmar) and Ceylon (Sri Lanka). It was not an easy task. The Assam Bengal Railway (ABR) remained with East Pakistan (now Bangladesh), along with India's entire north-eastern region, which was cut off from the rest of the country. Only 241 miles of India's entire route length was electrified, with the Bombay–Poona main line being the only electric route in the country. Most of the track was metre and broad gauge. The locomotive fleet was a mix of the old and the new, with several gauges and only a handful of diesels. Pre-1947, the total track mileage in India was around 52,000 miles. That impressive mileage was now reduced by 15,000, which was mostly conceded to Pakistan, a country created out of a need for a Muslim homeland. Routes, timetables, schedules and fares all had to be rewritten to meet the needs of the new governments. To aggravate matters, the disturbances that followed the partitioning grew into violent riots. Normal operations were suspended indefinitely and instead the railways began moving thousands of refugees both in and outside India. In the midst of chaos and anarchy, the railways also had to regroup on each side of the border. Employees, property, equipment and everything else had to be divided between the new states. When the dust finally settled down, India and Pakistan were each left with a fragment of what until then was one of the largest railway systems in the Indian subcontinent.

Given India's awe-inspiring size, the variety of gauges, the multitude of railway companies and the long period under British rule, it is understandably impossible to

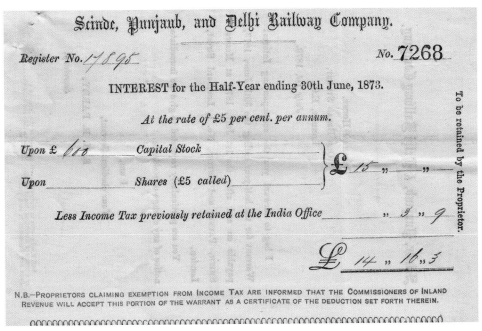

An interest statement issued by the Scinde, Punjab & Delhi Railway in 1873. Lucrative returns were promised on private capital invested in British-managed railway companies in India. The NWR constituent companies were paid up to 5 per cent on their money when placed under government control, in 1886. The government's share in the NWR eventually rose to 75 per cent, with the remaining 25 per cent co-owned by the government and the native princes. The NWR was also obliged to pay an additional 1 per cent to the Indian government and make up the loss resulting from the operation of the strategic Frontier lines.

refer in detail to every single steam locomotive that ever ran in the Raj. Thousands of locomotives were delivered to British India over the decades, with the majority coming from workshops in Glasgow (North British), Manchester (Beyer Peacock), Newcastle & Darlington (Robert Stephenson), Leeds (Kitson), Stafford (Bagnall) and, finally, from Newton-le-Willows (Vulcan Foundry). They ranged from the tiny 0-4-0s of the Darjeeling Railway to the enormous broad gauge Garratts. In between, there was a 'middle class' consisting of freight and passenger locomotives of all sizes. Other steam locomotives arrived from mainland Europe and America, although in smaller numbers.

At the beginning of the twentieth century, no other railway system on earth relied on more different locomotive types than that of India. A Locomotive Standardization Committee was therefore appointed in 1903. It was decided to create a catalogue of several official designs and let the railways choose the ones that suited them best. The committee specified 4-4-0 locomotives for passenger and 0-6-0 ones for freight services. Variations to each type were added in 1910 to deal with steeply graded routes that required more power. Further designs appeared in 1906: 4-6-0 and 4-4-2 for mail trains, 2-8-0 and 2-8-2T for heavy freight traffic and a passenger 2-6-4T. These standard types were known as BESA (British Engineering Standards Association) locomotives and were built in large numbers. An upsurge in post-1918 traffic resulted in a need for even more powerful locomotives. A second Locomotive Standards Committee was set up in 1924 to update the BESA designs and these came to be known as the Indian Railway Standards (IRS) locomotives.

The North-West Frontier Province

The North-West Frontier Province (NWFP) was established in November 1901 from the north-western districts of the Punjab Province. In 1947, it was divided between India and Pakistan. The NWFP included much of the current Khyber Province, excluding the Federally Administered Tribal Areas (FATA) and several princely states in that part of the Indian Empire. Its capital was the city of Peshawar. Until 1947, the province was bordered by five princely states to the north, the minor states of the Gilgit Agency to the north-east, the province of West Punjab to the east and the province of Baluchistan to the south. The Kingdom of Afghanistan lay more to the north-west.

The North-West Frontier areas were annexed to British India after the Second Sikh War (1848–49), in which British rule was established over the defeated Sikh kingdom. These newly won lands at first formed a part of the Punjab region until the creation of the NWFP in 1901. In 1955, the NWFP was merged into West Pakistan and renamed in 2010 as the Khyber Paktunkhwa Province.

British Baluchistan

Baluchistan is an arid and mountainous region covering the Pakistani province of Balochistan, the Iranian province of Sistan and the southern areas of Afghanistan, including Nimruz, Helmand and Kandahar provinces. It borders with the Pashtunistan region to the north, Sindh and Punjab to the east and Iran to the west. To the south

A 4-6-0 steam locomotive with a construction train on the Sind–Pishin State Railway, in a photo dated to 1886–89. The leading two wagons show many British design features, including the curved brake handle that was not used on main line wagons in Britain after the 1870s. Similarly, the van seems to be typically British and similar to vehicles built by Brown Marshalls of Adderley Park, Birmingham.

are the Arabian Sea and the Gulf of Oman. The provincial capital and largest city is Quetta. Largely underdeveloped, Baluchistan's economy rests on natural resources, such as natural gas, and Gwadar Port on the Arabian Sea.

In the 1870s, Baluchistan came under British colonial rule. In 1876, the British colonial administrator Sir Robert Sandeman negotiated the Treaty of Kalat, in which the princely states agreed to enter into a pact with the British government of India. The districts of Quetta, Pishin, Harnai, Sibi and Thal were similarly taken over by Britain in May 1879.

Two reasons determined the British colonial rule of Baluchistan. Protecting India's northern frontier from any potential invaders was as important as the need to secure the British hold of India. This is demonstrated in no uncertain terms in a report which appeared in *The Navy & Army Illustrated Magazine* on 8 March 1902. 'Of British Baluchistan, our control is absolute. Far beyond those limits, this influence extends and

A Double Fairle type steam locomotive in the Bolan Pass. Seventeen of these metre gauge 0-4-0+0-4-0T locomotives were built by the Avonside Engine Company in 1880. One was lost at sea. Originally ordered for the Bolan Pass, they ended up all over India and Burma.

the Baluch chiefs invariably prove amenable to the light but firm control which skilled and carefully-selected British agents exercise over them.' Reference is then made to the military value of the native population: 'The Baluch makes a first rate soldier and has done excellent work for us not only in India, but in such far-off regions as Uganda and China.' The advantage of controlling the region's trade routes was equally clear to the British: 'We occupy with a strong British garrison the fortress of Quetta, which commands the Bolan Pass. Years ago, a trade route was opened from Quetta to Persia and there is a steady and increasing stream of traffic. A railway now runs through the Bolan Pass to Chaman. In Quetta, there is a brisk trade in dried apricots and other products of the fertile Afghan valleys. There is a great future before Quetta, and one which is likely to receive careful developments in the hands of Indian statesmanship.' The Bolan Pass, so goes the report, 'is one of those forbidding passes which are a useful reminder that an invasion of India is not an enterprise to be taken lightly. This pleasing little gateway, which affords a good many advantages to a defending force, is surrounded by treeless and waterless country. It will be rightly regarded as effective a bulwark as many a continental fortress bristling with guns and strongly held by troops'.

The Punjab

The Punjab region is located in the northern part of the Indian subcontinent. Divided between Pakistan and India, its boundaries have changed repeatedly over the centuries.

NWR four-wheel inspection saloon coach. Note the chain firmly holding the right-side wheel to the track. Chaining the rolling stock to the rails was a simple and effective way of keeping the train from running away, probably as an extra precaution. Wooden shutters were used widely in India to protect the passengers from the strong glare of the sun.

An interesting combination of broad and narrow gauge stock. An NWR first class coach is attached to a Nowshera–Dargai Railway (Khyber Province) private car in a photo dated to 1903. The NDR was opened in 1901 and had a total length of 64 km. The private car in the photo is said to have been placed in the service of a British aristocrat on a visit to India.

In British India, it encompassed the present-day Indian states of Punjab, Haryana, Himachal Pradesh, Chandigarh and Delhi, along with the Pakistani regions of Punjab, Khyber-Pakhtunkhwa and Islamabad Capital Territory. To the west of the Punjab lies Baluchistan. Kashmir is to its north, the Hindi Belt is to the east and Rajasthan and Sindh are in the south. The region is often referred to as the breadbasket of both India and Pakistan.

One of the last areas of the Indian subcontinent to come under British rule, the Punjab was annexed in 1849. The province comprised five administrative divisions, Delhi, Jullundur, Lahore, Multan and Rawalpindi, and a number of princely states. In the 1947 Partition of India, it was carved up into East and West Punjab, in India and Pakistan.

The North Western Railway

'The tourist who has visited India will remember it as a mysterious land of temples, tigers, strange religious ceremonies, strong racial prejudices and glittering palaces.' This opening statement, from the April 1932 issue of the *Baldwin Locomotives Magazine*, accurately describes the adventures awaiting the first-time visitor to that country. The writer's next statement is equally correct and informative. 'If, however, we put romance aside and study our maps, we will discover that India is a land of railways. With a total of about 40,000 route miles of railways, India stands in fourth place among the countries of the world behind America, Russia and Canada. India has 2.5 times the population of the United States. More than 600 million passengers are carried annually, mostly in third class.' Comparing the situation in British India to America, the writer Malcolm K. Wright observes that 'there are many ways in which the railway problems of the two countries are similar. Long distances must be traversed; heavy grades and sharp curves are encountered in the mountainous districts; the difficulties of construction are similar, as deep gorges, swiftly flowing rivers and arid plains follow each other in rapid succession'. Mr Wright then observes that 'all of the parallels which we have drawn are particularly applicable in the case of the North Western Railway, which has the distinction of being the longest railway in India. Its 7,150 route miles stretch from Delhi on the east to the Persian border on the west; from Karachi on the south to the rugged mountain passes at Peshawar in the extreme northwest corner of India. More than 1,800 miles of the NWR are classed as strategic, having been built entirely for the defense of India against the traditional invaders of the northwest frontier'.

The North Western Railway of India was created on 1 January 1886 from the merger of several small companies. The Scinde, Punjab & Delhi Railway was amalgamated with the Indus Valley State Railway, the Punjab Northern State Railway, the Sind–Sagar Railway, the Sind–Pishin Railway and the Kandahar State Railway. Dozens of even smaller lines were also absorbed into the new administration. Essentially a commercial undertaking, the NWR was nonetheless conceived out of Britain's military concerns in central Asia. These concerns led to the construction of several strategic lines, such as the Bolan Pass Railway. Khojak Tunnel was opened in 1891, bringing the railway to Chaman, on the Afghan border. In 1947, much of the North Western Railway remained in Pakistan, becoming part of the Pakistan Western Railways. Across the border, in India, the other half of the NWR system was incorporated into the Eastern Punjab Railway. In 1952, it became a part of the Northern Railway, where it still remains.

Listed below are the constituent companies of the North Western Railway.

A hand-colored lantern slide showing a passenger train, with a dramatic view of the Louise Margaret Bridge on the Chappar Rift line, near Quetta. A hand-operated semaphore is visible at the entrance to the tunnel. (Library of Congress)

Sanzal station is located 19 km to the south-east of Chaman, on the way to Shela Bagh. Dominating the seemingly peaceful scene in this photo is the robust fort, next to the station building. Such forts were typical of the Frontier region and the hazardous tribal areas. (Library of Congress)

Scinde, Punjab & Delhi Railway (SPDR)

The SPDR was formed in 1870 from the incorporation of the Scinde Railway, the Indus Steam Flotilla, the Punjab Railway and the Delhi Railway. The Scinde Railway was established in March 1855 to construct a line between Karachi and Kotri. Work began in April 1858 and was completed on 13 May 1861, covering a distance of 174 km. The company was also involved in the establishment of the Indus Steam Flotilla, along the Indus and Chenab rivers.

Indus Valley State Railway (IVSR)

The IVSR was founded in 1871 to provide a rail link between Kotri and Multan, replacing the Indus Steam Flotilla. First surveyed in 1869, the new line connected Karachi with Lahore over the Empress Bridge and the mighty Sutlej River, which is the longest of the Punjab's five rivers. The IVSR reached the city of Rohri, on the eastern bank of the Indus River, in 1879. A steam ferry was provided to slowly transfer up to eight wagons to nearby Sukkur. It was not until 1889 and the opening of the Lansdowne Bridge that trains could finally travel directly between Karachi and Lahore. Today, this line is a section of the Pakistan Railways Karachi–Peshawar main route.

Punjab Northern State Railway (PNSR)

First proposed in 1857, construction of this so-called Lahore & Peshawar Railway was delayed for years due to political debate. Then in 1870, the PNSR was finally approved and built. The first section of the line was opened in 1876. In 1883, Attock Bridge, over the Indus River, was completed. It was one of several major bridges along the way to Peshawar, along with Jhelum River Bridge (1873); Alexandra Bridge, over the Chenab River between Wazirabad and Gujrat, which was officially opened in 1876 by King Edward VII; and Ravi River Bridge, between Sadiqpura, Lahore and Shahdara Bagh (1876).

Sind–Sagar Railway

Originally a metre gauge railway built to connect the Punjab city of Malakwal with the musically sounding town of Lala Musa (meaning Brother Moses). Serving a local salt mine, this railway was upgraded to broad gauge following the NWR merger of 1886 and designated as a Frontier Section military line.

Sind–Pishin State Railway (SPSR)

The SPSR connected Rohri with Chaman, on the approach to Afghanistan. Work on this scenic line commenced in October 1879 with a short section between Ruk and Sibi, at the entrance to the Nari Pass. The line was extended in 1880 as far as Pishin and the Harnai Pass, with the intention of reaching Afghanistan. The British plan to build a railway into Afghanistan was aborted in April 1881 and the construction of the line was therefore stopped. Two years later, however, it was decided to resume the work on the railway as part of the Harnai Road Improvement Scheme. Coming from Sibi, at a point located some 500 km from Karachi, the line entered the Nari Gorge through a tunnel and over a series of bridges. Reaching Harnai at an altitude of 2,950 feet, the line then climbed up to Dirgi, at 4,756 feet. Traversing the Chappar Rift was made possible over the Louise Margaret Bridge, whose magnificent remains are a popular travel destination in modern-day Pakistan.

Heavily damaged in floods and land slips, the line was rebuilt along the new route of the Mushkaf-Bolan Railway. Descending from Kachh, it reached Khanai (5,487 feet) and Bostan (5,154 feet), where it joined the Bolan Railway from Quetta and turned north towards Khojak and Chaman. The Bostan–Chaman section was opened in January 1888, reaching Chaman in January 1892.

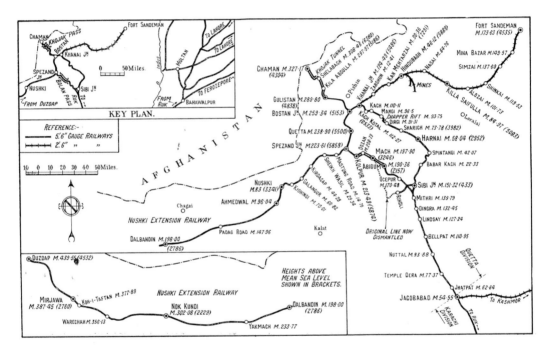

The Quetta Division is clearly shown in this map of the NWR broad and narrow gauge lines in the Indian Frontier area. Also shown is the Nushki Extension Railway to Duzdap (now Zahedan) in Iran.

Trans Baluchistan Railway

Technically not one of the constituent railways that merged to form the NWR in 1886, the Quetta–Taftan Railway is today one of the four main railway lines in Pakistan. With twenty-three stops along the way from Quetta to Iran, this line is 523 km long and goes as far as Zahedan, at the Iranian border. The Trans Baluchistan Railway was a military route linking British India with Iran. The first section, from Quetta to Nushki, was approved as early as August 1902 and inaugurated in November 1905. The remainder of the line, to the west of Nushki, was named the Nushki Extension Railway. It terminated at the Iranian town of Duzdap (today called Zahedan), which was disconnected from the rest of the Iranian railway system until 2009. Known as the Lonely Line, it was the loneliest railway in the entire subcontinent. Between Dalbandin and Nok Kundi, 170 km apart, there was only one intermediate station – Yakmach – in the entire wilderness. Traffic on this line was modest indeed, with only two passenger trains per week between Quetta and Zahedan and an occasional freight train. A decline in the need for a railway along that route led to the temporary closure of the section between Kundi and Zahedan in 1931, with the track lifted. Following the outbreak of the Second World War in 1939, the hitherto dismantled Quetta–Zahedan line was rebuilt and reopened on 20 April 1940.

In 1879, twenty-five Double Fairlie type steam locomotives were ordered for the North Western Frontier, in connection with the Third Afghan War. The order was withdrawn in 1880, but seventeen of the locomotives were ready and these became Indian State Railways 361–377. One locomotive was lost at sea, and another was sold to a Bombay contractor. The remaining fifteen were finally shipped off to work on the Bolan Pass. They then remained in store from 1887, when ten went to Burma in 1896. Four others ended up with the Nilgiri Mountain Railway in 1907 as NMR 1–4. One of the ex-Bolan Pass Fairlie locomotives is seen with a passenger train near Coonoor, on the Nilgiri line.

In 1888, the NWR experimented with back-to-back locomotives. Twenty Class TG 0-6-0 'Sandiford twins' (after Charles Sandiford, the locomotive superintendent) arrived from Glasgow (Neilson 3766–3785/NWR 206–225), which were operated in pairs, backing on to a common tender. They were not a success on the severe gradients for which they were designed and were eventually assigned to singly haul ordinary freight trains for the remainder of their career in India.

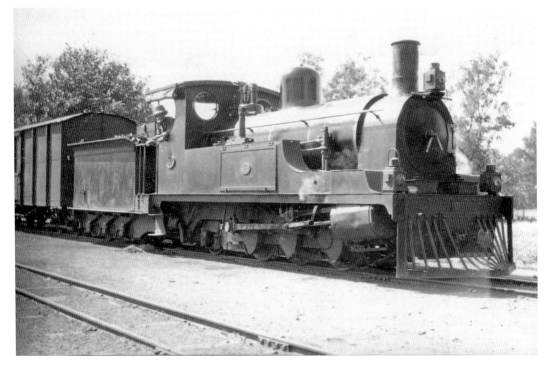

NWR 0-6-2 steam locomotive No. 86 (Kitson 3972 of 1900) began life as Nowshera–Dargai State Railway No. 6, in what is now Pakistan. Six locomotives were delivered to the NDR in two batches of three each. The tank-like structure above the locomotive's running plate was especially designed to protect the valve gear. The line was converted to broad gauge in 1921–22. One locomotive is known to have ended up with the Saraya Sugar Mill near Gorakphur, in India, which operated a variety of narrow gauge steam locomotives.

In British Baluchistan, the Mushkaf–Bolan Railway was the third attempt to construct a railway through the Bolan Pass. The line formed an alternative route to the Sind–Pishin State Railway. This official works photo shows American-made NWR Class TAA 2-8-2T steam locomotive No. 196 (Pittsburgh Locomotive & Car Works 2231 of 1901). The eight members of this class were numbered 189–196 and renumbered 675–682. They were built for use on the Chaman incline, leading to Afghanistan.

Pakistan Railways

At the time of the Partition of India in 1947, Pakistan consisted of two geographically separated territories, to the east and west of India. East Pakistan became Bangladesh in 1974. West Pakistan, which is the subject of this book, became the Islamic Republic of Pakistan. The story of the railways in Pakistan begins in 1861, with the opening of a line from Karachi to Kotri, on the Indus River. In the following years, a rapidly growing railway system emerged on both sides of the Indus. Serving the region was the Indus Valley State Railway, alongside other railway companies. In accordance with a condition imposed by the British Governor General, Lord Dalhousie, the gauge chosen for the railway was 1,676 mm (broad gauge). Confronted with a possible Russian invasion of India, the creation of the North Western Railway, in 1886, was a part of Britain's strategic attempt to repel any military threat from the north. By then, there were close to 3,000 km of railways in that part of British India. In 1947, that number rose to 11,000 km of railway lines, primarily in the province of Punjab and the future West Pakistan. This included the Quetta line and various British military extensions dating back to the First World War. A whole lot of tunnels and bridges were needed to overcome the extremely challenging topography in the frontier area, where heavy floods remain a major concern right down to this day. Cost-cutting narrow gauge lines were also built in the mountainous areas. One outstanding examples of these lines was the metre gauge line out of Hyderabad, which was subsequently converted to broad gauge. The other example was the Bostan–Zhob (formerly Fort Sandeman) line, along with several 762 mm branch lines afoot the Afghan mountains.

SPDR 0-4-2 No. 47 *EAGLE* was built in Britain in 1871. The oldest surviving locomotive in Pakistan, it is now preserved outside Moghulpura workshops in Lahore.

NWR HGS class 2-8-0 locomotive No. 1728 (later renumbered 2178) was built by Kitson of Leeds under the works number 5066. It was the first in a large order placed with Kitson for forty-eight heavy goods locomotives in 1914. The HGS class eventually totalled 133 locomotives. NWR Nos 1728–1775 (Kitson Nos 5066–5113) were all taken over by Pakistan in 1947. This elegant locomotive was placed on static display in the Punjab town of Alipur Chatha, to the north of Lahore, formerly on the NWR Wazirabad–Lyallpur line. It was sadly scrapped in 2003.

NWR HB class locomotive No. 185 (later renumbered 629) had an unsurprisingly Scottish appearance, given its provenance. It was built by Neilson of Glasgow in 1901, as their works number 5774. The ten locomotives of this class (NWR Nos 179–188, renumbered 623–632) were Neilson Nos 5768–77. They were the last of the outside-cylindered 4-4-0s before the introduction, a year later, of the M class, which had larger wheels. (ETH Collection)

Another order placed with Neilson in 1888 was for five locomotives for use on the Chaman line. These powerful NWR Class TB 0-8-0STs were originally numbered 201–205 before becoming 687–691. Their Neilson works numbers were 3760–3764. (ETH Collection)

Official works photos of NWR narrow gauge locomotives are rare indeed. NWR steam locomotive No. 143 was built by the North British Locomotive Company under the NBL works number 21084 of 1915. Five of these 4-6-2s were delivered to the Khushalgarh–Kohat–Tal Railway, which was a 762 mm British military frontier line opened in 1902. All five became NWR Class P 141–145, then Class Q in April 1929. The final two out of the five were Kitson Nos 5174–5 of 1918.

According to the 1922 Railway Yearbook, the NWR maintained a fleet of 1,627 steam locomotives with 3,537 coaches, 30,574 freight cars, sixteen railcars and fifteen road vehicles. Also listed in the book are notable NWR engineering works: 'Lansdowne Bridge, Sukkur – one span of 906 ft., one of 270 ft., and one of 230 ft. Kotri Bridge – five spans of 250 ft. and one of 100 ft. Attock Bridge – two spans of 296 ft. and three of 246 ft. Wazirabad Bridge – seventeen spans of 133 ft. and Khojak Tunnel – 2.5 miles.' In the decades that followed the demise of the British rule of India, much has changed in Pakistan. Diesels have long since taken over from the steam locomotives of the pre-partition era. Most of the NWR infrastructure remained in Pakistan and was renamed the Pakistan Western Railway. The country inherited a little more than 8,000 km of the North Western State Railway, 6,880 km of which was of 1,676 mm broad gauge, 506 km of metre gauge and 736 km of 762 mm narrow gauge. In 1954, a new extension was built from the Karachi–Peshawar main line to Mardan and Charsada. Two years later, in 1956, the Jacobabad–Kashmore Railway was converted to broad gauge. The Kot Adu–Kashmore section of the Kotri–Attock line was completed in 1973, providing an alternative route from Karachi to northern Pakistan. 293 km of track, between Khanewal and Lahore, were electrified in 1966, but the twenty-nine electric locomotives (PR 7001–29) have been reported as held in storage owing to the theft of the copper overhead power lines. The 762 mm gauge lines had all vanished. In 1997, there were seventy-nine broad gauge and eighteen metre gauge steam locomotives left in Pakistan, with 533 diesels and five railcars. Pakistan's international rail links include the Zahedan line to Iran and a proposed line from Chaman to Kandahar, in Afghanistan, and onwards to Turkmenistan. Another proposal would extend the Karachi–Peshawar line to Kabul via Jalalabad. A feasibility study of a new line to China is under review. Finally, there are two links to India.

The Thar Express connects Jodhpur with Karachi and the Samjhauta (meaning 'agreement' and 'compromise' in both Hindi and Urdu) Express is in service between Delhi and Lahore. It is worth mentioning here that The Thar is named after the giant Thar Desert. Both services were established on the basis of the 1972 Simla Agreement and the restoring of the Jodhpur–Hyderabad rail route, which was closed for forty-one years until 2006.

Predominately an area of British military activity, the North Western Frontier also had a romantic appeal. Visitors to this forsaken part of India were drawn to the solitude of the desert and the beauty of the land, as depicted in this Indian State Railways poster showing a passenger train in the Khyber Pass.

Two examples of accidents and incidents on the NWR. This dramatic view shows the aftermath of a nasty head-on collision near Ludhiana on 27 December 1907. The locomotives involved in this violent crash were both M class 4-4-0s, with one identified as NWR No. 802, which was built by Sharp Stewart in 1902.

Another Frontier area accident was reported in the *Times of India*, showing what could be the unfortunate results of a runaway train near Quetta. Note the steam locomotive parked in the background. Numerous railway accidents occurred both in the North Western Province as well as in Pakistan, as recently as October 2019 when a passenger train was destroyed in fire while travelling from Karachi to Rawalpindi.

Khyber Pass

Located on the ancient Silk Road in central Asia, the Khyber Pass connects Afghanistan with the Valley of Peshawar, in northern Pakistan. Since ancient times the gateway to India, its summit is at Landi Kotal, 5 km inside Pakistan, on the descent to Jamrud.

Mounting British military concerns over the situation in the North-West Frontier were proven right in 1878, with the outbreak of the Second Anglo-Afghan War. Seeking a way to better secure India's border with Afghanistan, in 1879 a new line was proposed across the Khyber Pass, from Peshawar to Landi Khana and Landi Kotal. Begun in 1905, it was not until the outbreak of the Third Anglo-Afghan War in May 1919 that the section between Jamrud and Landi Kotal was completed, on 3 November 1925. It was extended in 1926 to Landi Khana, a distance of 8 km, stopping short of Afghanistan itself. The railway climbed up a height of 2,000 feet along the way from Jamrud to Landi Kotal, with a drop of 872 feet down the last stretch to Landi Khana. That single line, which was the last major railway project in the British-ruled frontier area, had four reversing stations, thirty-four tunnels, ninety-two bridges and culvers and four locomotive watering stations. Post-1947, a weekly passenger train continued to run through the Khyber Pass as a statement of authority on the part of the new Pakistani government. Even before that, under political pressure from Afghanistan, the short section connecting Landi Kotal with Landi Khana was closed down on 15 December 1932. Traffic in the Khyber Pass survived the Partition of India for a few more decades until 1982, when all regular services were stopped. The track was damaged by flooding in 2006, 2007 and again in 2008. With operations suspended indefinitely, a Khyber Pass revival may only happen as part of a new railway connecting Pakistan with Afghanistan.

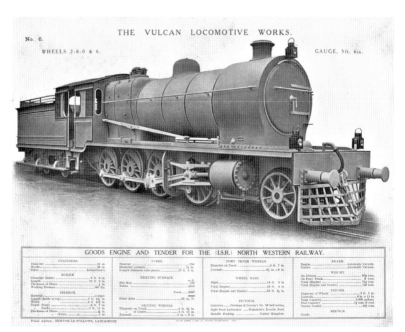

NWR locomotives in official manufacturer catalogues. This photo shows one of the HG class 2-8-0s, which were built by Vulcan Foundry in 1907–08 (NWR Nos 1516–1555, VF works numbers 2260–2279 and 2240–2259).

BEYER, PEACOCK & CO. LTD.   MANCHESTER, ENGLAND

| EAST INDIAN RAILWAY | TYPE 2-8-2 T | SERVICE — GENERAL PURPOSE | No. 02371 |

Five Class HST (BESA general purpose) 2-8-2T steam locomotives were built for the NWR by Beyer Peacock at their Gorton works in Manchester in 1924 (NWR Nos 203–207/BP Nos 6173–6177). HT stands for Heavy Tank. This was the last type of BESA locomotives introduced in India. Curiously, the locomotive depicted, NWR No. 203, is described as having belonged to the East Indian Railway (EIR). This could be explained by the fact that in the same year, EIR took delivery of identical Beyer Peacock locomotives (EIR Nos 1612–1641/BP Nos 6140–6169).

The frontier lines near Quetta were steep enough as to call for some creative thinking. In 1887, two Abt 0-6-2T steam locomotives were ordered from the German manufacturer Maschinenfabrik Esslingen to be used on a short rack section of the Bolan Pass railway. The pair was originally numbered 1 and 2 and then 714 and 715. When a new line on an easier gradient was completed, they were both downgraded to yard switchers. Their Esslingen works numbers were 2230 and 2231.

The only known photo of a rack locomotive in north-western India. NWR No. 714 (Esslingen No. 2230 of 1887) was built in Germany for use on a steep section of Bolan Pass line. This photo appears to have been taken after the locomotive became a yard switcher, following the introduction of stronger locomotives on the Quetta route. (IRFCA collection)

The 762 mm gauge Jacobabad–Kashmore Railway was opened in 1914, off the Rohri–Bolan Pass main line. Also called the Upper Sind Light Railway, the JKR was operated by the NWR. The line was purchased by the government of India in 1945 and passed to Pakistan on partition in 1947. Seen in a vintage Société Franco-Belge (Belgium) rolling stock catalogue is JKR 2-6-2 steam locomotive No. 4, which later on became NWR S Class 170 (FB NO. 2339 of 1924). This type of locomotive was the forerunner for the narrow gauge ZB class.

Official works photo of NWR MAS class, mallet type 2-6-6-2 steam locomotive No. 460 (Baldwin Locomotive Works 56380). A single example of this American giant of the rails was purchased in 1923 for comparison with NWR No. 480, a Garratt locomotive ordered from Beyer Peacock in 1925. Both locomotives were tested on the Bolan Pass section, between Sibi and Quetta, where they constantly suffered from wheel slippage. They were then transferred to the less graded section between Lala Musa and Rawalpindi. Of the Baldwin locomotive, it has been reported that a spanner was accidentally left in one of its low-pressure cylinders, leading to the untimely loss of the whole locomotive due to the shortage of spare parts. Both Garratt and mallet were scrapped before partition.

By the 1920s the cost of importing British coal to India was becoming prohibitive, forcing a switch to low quality, locally produced coal. A new standard series of locomotive designs was prepared with wider fireboxes, including the front-line express type, the XC class 4-6-2. NWR No. 241 was the second of two locomotives built in 1928 by Vulcan Foundry (works number 4141). It was renumbered 1841 in 1930. The XC and related XB class Pacifics performed poorly and a special committee, which included Sir William Stanier of the LMS, travelled to India to recommend many design modifications. (Keith Chester collection)

NWR XA2 class locomotive No. 2703 at Nowshera. Eight of these 4-6-2s arrived from the Great Indian Peninsula Railway in 1936 due to the electrification of parts of the GIPR system. NWR No. 2703 (ex-GIPR No. 2202) was built by Vulcan Foundry in 1929 as works number 4273.

Partly due to the problems with the XC class, several Indian railways built small numbers of express locomotives to non-standard designs in the 1930s. On the NWR this included four four-cylinder Pacifics classified XS, all slightly different. NWR Nos 760 and 761 were classified XS1 and had Caprotti valve gear, while Nos 780 and 781 had Lentz gear and were XS2. The even-numbers examples of both classes had the inside cylinders at 135° to the outside cylinders, while 761 and 781 had the usual 180°. All were built by Vulcan Foundry in 1930, and were very successful on the crack Delhi–Lahore–Karachi expresses, continuing until dieselization in Pakistan in the 1960s. NWR XS2 class No. 780 (VF No. 4295) is shown at Lahore MPD, probably in the early 1930s as the smoke deflectors were later removed. (Keith Chester collection)

"BEYER-GARRATT" PATENT ARTICULATED LOCOMOTIVES

INDIAN STATE (NORTH WESTERN RAILWAY)

5′ 6″ Gauge   Design No. **111**

TRACTIVE EFFORT : { at **75%** Boiler Pressure **47,110** lb. / at **85%** ,, ,, **53,390** lb.   MAXIMUM AXLE LOAD **19·5** TONS.

Cylinders (**4**), diameter × stroke **18½″ × 26″**	Boiler Heating Surface :	Grate Area .. .. .. **56·5** sq. ft.
Coupled wheels, diameter .. **4′ 3″**	Tubes .. .. .. **2469** sq. ft.	Fuel Capacity (Coal) .. **11** tons.
Boiler Pressure .. .. **180** lb./sq.″	Firebox .. .. .. **235** ,,	Water Capacity .. **6,500** gallons.
Wheel Base, each unit .. **23′ 0″**	Total Evaporative .. **2704** ,,	Adhesive Weight in working
,, ,, rigid .. .. **11′ 0″**	Superheater .. .. **550** ,,	order .. .. .. **115·4** tons.
,, ,, total .. .. **72′ 0″**	Total .. .. .. **3254** ,,	Total Weight in working order **178·4** ,,

Factor of Adhesion, in working order, **5·5** (**75%** B.P.) **4·85** (**85%** B.P.).

An important and extremely difficult section of the North Western Railway broad gauge system runs through the Bolan Pass between Sibi and Kolpur, a distance of 62 miles. Rising from Sibi the line has a grade of 1 in 55 for 39 miles until Ab-i-gum is reached, when the grade changes to 1 in 33 for 7½ miles. At Much the most severe part of the journey is commenced as the line has for the remaining 15¾ miles to Kolpur a continuous climb of 1 in 25 ; the Railway running through country necessitating constant curvature.

Only one Garratt locomotive was ever built for the North Western Railway. Numbered 480, this GAS class 2-6-2+2-6-2 was built by Beyer Peacock of Manchester as works number 6203 of 1925. It was tested on the Bolan Pass line as a possible replacement for the four HGS class 2-8-0s which were normally needed to haul the trains up the heavy gradient to Quetta. The Garratt was able to haul about 30 tons more load than a pair of ordinary 2-8-0s. It was then transferred to the Rawalpindi section for more performance tests. However, the situation changed with the arrival of thirty powerful 2-10-0 locomotives from the Great Indian Peninsula Railway. The single NWR Garratt was thus retired in 1937, only twelve years after entering service in India.

Beyer Peacock-built NWR Garratt No. 480. A well-designed locomotive, it was equipped with superheating and Belpaire firebox and tested against a Baldwin mallet. Both Garratt and mallet were ultimately rejected in favour of the standard 2-8-0 type. (IRFCA collection)

Bolan Pass

'The Bolan Pass proper, with the narrow winding defile through the Dozan Gorge, comes between Hirok and Kolpur. Crossing the ravine nine times in four miles and burrowing through the rocky crags which tower high above the stony bed, the railway construction is a succession of mighty girder bridges and tunnels. There is a rugged grandeur about this sinister place. In the days of steam the sight and sound of four lusty Consolidations working a nine-coach Mail up the five miles of almost uninterrupted climb at the rate of one foot rise in every twenty-five were things no railwayman is ever likely to forget.' (P. S. A. Berridge, *Couplings to the Khyber*)

The Bolan Pass is a long mountain pass in western Pakistan, 120 km from the border with Afghanistan. Made up of narrow gorges, the pass connects Sibi with Quetta both by road and rail. Considered to this day as one of the greatest feats in British India, the Bolan Pass line is an engineering wonder. A railway through the Bolan Pass was first proposed in 1876 and completed as far as Quetta in August 1886. In 1889, the original line was swept away in a flood, so much so that the railway had to be rebuilt well above the riverbed. The new line was inaugurated on 15 April 1897 and is still in service. From Sibi, the line goes through seventeen tunnels and repeatedly crosses the Bolan River as it approaches Quetta. In 1887, the railway connected Karachi in the south with Quetta in the north through the Bolan Pass and the picturesque Chappar Rift. Both were replaced by the new Mushkaf–Bolan route in 1895, opening up the way for the Bolan Mail. The demanding climb up the mighty Bolan Pass to Quetta necessitated the use of up to four steam locomotives. With the arrival of new locomotives in Pakistan, the Bolan Mail was placed in the charge of ALCO diesels. Immediately behind the locomotive, armed guards were housed in a converted boxcar to protect the train from the lawless tribesmen in the area.

NWR SG class locomotive No. 122x with a passenger train at Hasan Abdal station (Punjab), 40 km to the north-west of Islamabad. The locomotive was only five years old when this photo was taken in 1916. These little 0-6-0s were popular throughout the NWR system, with multiple orders placed with North British and Vulcan Foundry.

Old (1869) and New X.C. Class Locomotives, North Western Railway.

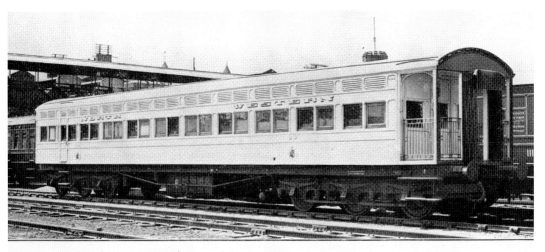

First-Class Tourist Saloon No. 39, North Western Railway.

Previous page bottom, this page above and below: Various views of NWR steam locomotives and rolling stock, as described in the captions.

Locomotive Shed at Multan, North Western Railway

The NWR headquarters were located at Lahore, the capital of the Punjab. With a workforce of 10,000 men, the railway workshops were located at Moghalpura, 3 miles to the east of Lahore. The erecting shop accommodated up to seventy-eight locomotives, with 500 heavy repairs carried out per year. This historical photo shows Lahore locomotive shed in 1929.

Chappar Rift

On 27 March 1885 another route was opened to Quetta via Harnai, Khost and Bostan. This was the Chappar Rift railway, a masterpiece of engineering which was sadly replaced with another route and abandoned.

The Chappar Rift is a huge fissure running at right angles from one valley to another, across the surrounding mountains. Taking advantage of this natural phenomenon, the railway was built along a shelf below the towering precipices and along the entire length of the Rift. Coming from the south, the train negotiated a horseshoe curve across the valley and climbed up the hillside into a rock tunnel, emerging on the Louise Margaret Bridge, at the height of 230 feet above the ground. It then proceeded through a series of tunnels to a valley below Mangi station. The ruling gradient on this spectacular line was 1 in 40, with a maximum altitude of nearly 6,000 feet above sea level. The plan to build a railway through the Chappar Rift required the best skills of the engineers who were put in charge of this ambitious project. Overcoming the topography of the Rift was one thing, but to further complicate matters, 8 kilometres of the line were built along a mud gorge. Rich with soft gypsum, the gorge floor proved too weak to hold the track in position, resulting in the displacement and sinking of a tunnel portal. The solution found was to lift the track to a sufficiently safe level above the gorge.

The highlight of the Chappar Rift line and its chief engineering feature was the Louise Margaret Bridge. It was named after Princess Louise Margaret of Prussia, who became the Duchess of Connaught upon marrying Prince Arthur, Duke of Connaught and Strathearn, in 1879. Inaugurated by the duchess during her stay to India, the effort involved in the design and actual construction of this bridge was second to none. Its highest pier stood 90 feet tall and the weight of the iron girders alone was 600 tons. The bridge consisted of seven short spans, 40 feet each, and a long span of 150 feet, which was placed right over the deepest part of the creek below.

The Chappar Rift railway provided access to Quetta for a little over half a century. Then on the night of 10 July 1942, the line was swept away in a flash flood, which destroyed the track in the Rift and eroded the foundations. The condition of the line was then evaluated. With only one train a week between Zardalu and Bostan, in 1943 it was decided to close down that section. The decision was carried out in the same year and the track was dismantled, with the steel spans of the Louise Margaret Bridge.

New 2-8-2 steam locomotives being unloaded from the MV *Clan MacDougall*. The ship is reported as having been sunk by a German U-boat in May 1941, suggesting that the photo was taken in 1929, showing Vulcan Foundry-built XE class locomotives for the North Western and East Indian Railways.

NWR XG class steam locomotive No. 911 (Beyer Peacock No. 6505 of 1928). Originally built as 0-8-0 locomotives, in 1943 the three members of this small class were converted in Mughalpura into 2-8-2s. They were used on the NWR and later on the Eastern Punjab Railway as yard switchers. NWR No. 911 is now on static display at the National Railway Museum in New Delhi.

NWR XA class No. 261 was the first of two 4-6-2s built by Vulcan Foundry in 1929 (VF Nos 4158–4159). It was later renumbered 2651. Designed for branch line passenger services, the XAs were the smallest of the three Pacific IRS types, with an axle load of 13 tons. 113 were delivered to various broad gauge railways in India. Replacing the older NWR L class 4-6-0s, the new XA Pacifics were used to haul trains up the Chappar Rift line to Quetta.

The NWR 4-6-2 locomotive in this photo, either NWR No. 760 or No. 761, was built by Vulcan Foundry in 1930. It is here seen standing on a turntable.

Forty-four XE class 2-8-2s were ordered for India from William Beardmore and another forty-nine from Vulcan Foundry between 1928 and 1945. NWR locomotive No. 221 was Vulcan Foundry No. 4145 of 1928. The type was the largest of the unarticulated steam locomotives ever used on Indian Railways. Weighing up to 200 tons in working order, they were capable of reaching a speed of 30 mph. The 2-8-2 wheel arrangement was provided to reduce the axle load, which stood at 22.5 tons per axle when fully loaded. In the 1947 partition, thirty-five XE locomotives went to Pakistan, with fifty-eight left in India.

A German in India. NWR No. 229 is an example of non-British steam locomotive orders for service in pre-partition India. The Hannoversche Maschinenbau AG, better known as Hanomag, supplied the NWR with twelve ZE class (762 mm narrow gauge) 2-8-2s in 1930. NWR No. 229 was Hanomag works number 10740. Four members of this class, Nos 230–232 and 234, all built by Hanomag in 1930, are preserved in Pakistan.

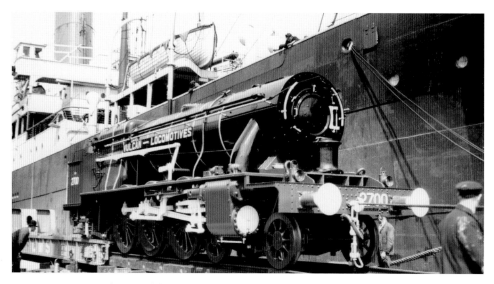

From Britain to the world. Exporting steam locomotives to all four corners of the globe was once a leading industry in Britain. NWR XA1 class locomotive No. 2700 (Vulcan Foundry No. 4527 of 1931) is seen on the start of its long voyage to India. 113 broad gauge XA Pacifics were built for India, all by VF between 1929 and 1935. The Indian examples were largely out of use by the end of 1979. A total of thirty-seven went to Pakistan at partition, a few of these surviving into the 1990s.

Vulcan Foundry-built NWR XA class locomotive No. 2662 (VF No. 4369 of 1929) en route to the docks aboard a Marston Road Services low-loader.

No. 22.

THE VULCAN LOCOMOTIVE WORKS.

STANDARD PASSENGER ENGINE AND TENDER

FOR THE

(I.S.R.) NORTH WESTERN RAILWAY.

(FITTED WITH PHŒNIX SUPERHEATER.)

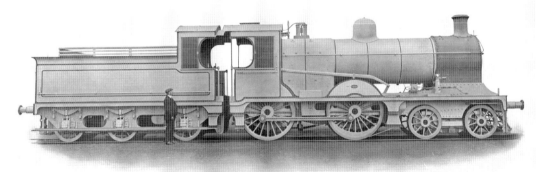

A page from a Vulcan Foundry catalogue showing one of the many 4-4-0 locomotives which were built for India before 1914. The example in this photo was superheated. Construction of SPS class locomotives for the NWR started in 1911.

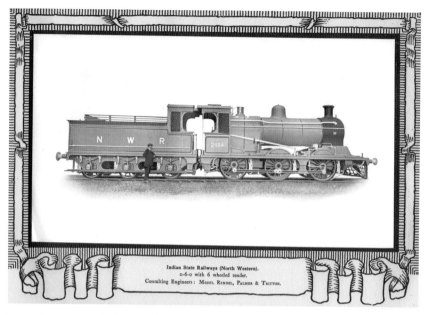

Indian State Railways (North Western).
o-6-o with 6 wheeled tender.
Consulting Engineers: Messrs. Rendel, Palmer & Tritton.

Seen in an Armstrong Whitworth steam locomotives catalogue is NWR locomotive No. 2484. Twenty-three of these Elswick, Newcastle SGS class 0-6-0s were built for the NWR in 1922. Their road numbers were 2484–2506 (Armstrong Whitworth 137–159).

Kitson-Meyer Articulated Locomotive, Kalka-Simla Railway. Built by Kitson & Co. Ltd., Leeds.

SCALE = HALF SIZE

Tyre Profile of Kitson-Meyer Locomotive.

General View of Engine Bogie.

One of India's beloved hill railways, the Kalka–Shimla Railway requires little introduction. Once under NWR administration, the KSR owned a pair of TS class, Kitson-Meyer type 2-6-2+2-6-2 steam locomotives built in 1928 under the Kitson works numbers 5413 and 5414. This photo shows the locomotive side view and one of the two powered bogies.

A KSR survivor at the National Railway Museum, New Delhi. NWR locomotive No. 78 is a ZF class 2-6-2T built by the Kassel, Germany, firm of Henschel in 1935 as works number 22589. It later became All India No. 107.

The Frontier Mail passing over a viaduct on the Darah section of the Bombay, Baroda & Central India Railway. It was one of British India's first-class trains, carrying passengers to Delhi, Lahore, Rawalpindi and Peshawar. The level of comfort on this train was second to none in the country. The train was made up of BBCIR and NWR coaches on alternate days. Until 1940, it comprised of six coaches, including a restaurant car. In 1996, the Frontier Mail was rechristened as The Golden Temple Mail. It currently covers a total distance of 1,891 km from Mumbai Central to Amritsar, in the process crossing seven states on the way to Punjab.

November 11, 1929. THE RAILWAY GAZETTE. 19

THE FRONTIER MAIL.

The
Royal Mail Route

TO **DELHI** AND THE **PUNJAB**

Bombay—Delhi $23\frac{1}{2}$ *hours.*

INDIA'S FASTEST DAILY TRAIN SERVICE.

Direct weekly connecting services with P. & O. Mail Steamers
from and to Europe.

TRAVEL IN SPEED AND COMFORT BY
THE

B.B. & C.I.Ry

The Punjab Mail (also known as the Punjab Limited) was another deluxe, long-distance train in India. With six cars in tow and a seating capacity for ninety-six passengers, the train departed directly from Ballard Pier Mole in Bombay on the long voyage to Delhi and the North-West Frontier. In 1914, the originating station was shifted to Victoria Terminus. After the Partition of India in 1947, the train terminated at the border town of Firozpur, on the banks of the Sutlej River.

BOMBAY BARODA & CENTRAL INDIA RAILWAY
Pacific Type Express Locomotive No. 603
Mr. F. J. Page, Locomotive Superintendent.
Messrs. Rendel, Palmer & Tritton, Consulting Engineers.
Built by The Vulcan Foundry, Ltd., Newton-le-Willows.

Seventy-two XC class locomotives were built in Britain between 1928 and 1931. Forty of them were ordered from Vulcan Foundry in 1928–29. Of the VF locomotives, only two were built for the NWR (VF Nos 4140–4141, NWR Nos 240–241). NWR took delivery of another twenty-six XC locomotives from William Beardmore in 1930–31. This fine photo shows BBCIR XC locomotive No. 603 (Vulcan Foundry No. 4142 of 1928). The Frontier Mail's total journey time was shortened thanks to the outstanding performance of these elegant locomotives on the Bombay–Delhi line. There is, however, evidence suggesting that the XCs suffered from a whole lot of mechanical problems and were not exactly as advertised.

The Karachi mail leaving Lahore, North Western Railway of India
4-cyl. simple 4-6-2 locomotive No. 780, with R.C. poppet valve gear

The Karachi Mail leaving Lahore in 1934 behind NWR XS2 class locomotive No. 780.

Resembling a medieval castle, Lahore station was designed by civil engineer William Burton in 1859. It is here seen in one of the earliest known photos of the station building. The sharp-eyed reader will notice the letters SPDR marked on the white roofed baggage car, immediately below the wide portal. (DC collection)

A recent view of Lahore station, taken in September 2014. The station presently serves as the Pakistan Railways headquarters. Plinthed outside the formidable walls is narrow gauge ZB class locomotive No. 205 (Hanomag No. 10761 of 1932). (Wikimedia Commons)

INTERIOR VIEW OF RAILWAY STATION, RAWAL PINDI.   No. 27.

Rawalpindi station was opened in 1881, during the construction of the Punjab Northern State Railway. It is one of several major stops on the main line between Karachi and Peshawar. Under British rule, Rawalpindi flourished as a large commercial centre. It has since then grown to become Pakistan's fourth largest city. This photo, believed taken in the 1920s, shows a passenger train next to the station building on a rainy day.

The beautiful architecture of Karachi station in a photo from the golden era of the British colonial rule in India. Construction of the station began in 1896 and was completed in 1898. The station building was declared a protected heritage site by the local authorities.

A photo taken shortly after the completion of Khojak Tunnel, near Quetta. NWR HL Class ('Heavy L') 4-6-0 locomotive No. 387 was built by Neilson of Glasgow in 1886.

Regular steam on the Bolan Pass. Smartly turned out Pakistan Western Railway (ex-NWR) HGS class 2-8-0 locomotive No. 2204 emerges from the ornate summit tunnel entrance at Kolpur station with a passenger train in 1970. No. 2204 was built by Kitson of Leeds in 1914 as works number 5092.

Set in the dry desert, the short-lived line from Landi Khana to Landi Kotal, in the Khyber Pass, was opened in 1926 and abandoned in 1932. The British plan to extend this strategic railway to Kabul was met with opposition on the other side of the border with Afghanistan and was finally dropped.

The Lahore–Quetta train in the 1930s, hauled by three HGS class 2-8-0 locomotives. The location is Nannar Nala Bridge, at the beginning of the Bolan Pass incline.

Special Series No. 82   TRAIN COMING OUT OF A TUNNEL ON
KHYBER RAILWAY, N.W.F.P.

A scene from bygone days in Pakistan. An NWR 2-8-0 locomotive heads a freight train out of a tunnel in the Khyber Pass. The photo is dated to 1918. Sixty years later, in 1978, the service was down to one weekly train, a Friday-only service that ran to take passengers to the market at Landi Kotal. The train only ran with three, mostly empty coaches. This service ceased sometime in the 1990s. An attempt was made to run a regular tourist train through the Khyber Pass, but the deteriorating security situation in the region saw the last charter trips run towards the end of 2005.

The Sibi–Harnai–Quetta line was the first to successfully connect Quetta with the rest of India. The first train steamed into Quetta via Harnai in 1887. This glass slide shows a passenger train at Kach station, near the divide between Harnai and Quetta. The locomotive appears to be fitted with a snow plough.

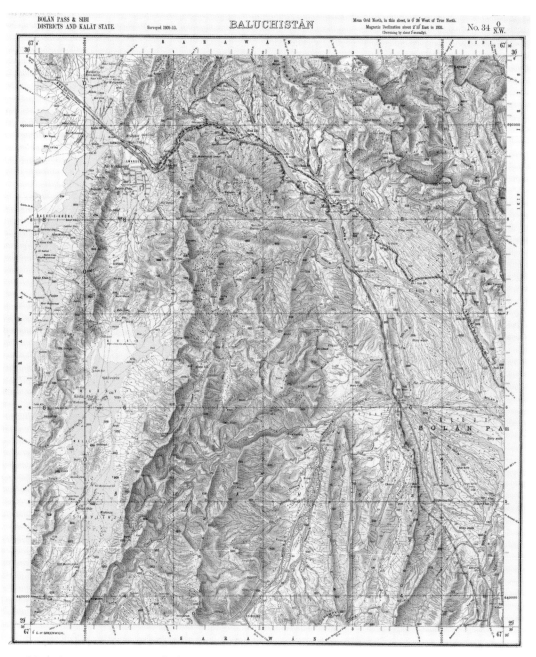

Little imagination is needed to appreciate the immense challenge posed by the natural obstacles during the design and actual construction of the Bolan Pass line. This detailed map, issued in 1916, shows the line as it follows the Bolan River, on the way to Quetta.

OUT OF ONE TUNNEL AND INTO ANOTHER

ALI MASJID GORGE

GIRDER BRIDGE OVER A LOOP IN THE MOTOR ROAD

CONSTRUCTION TRAIN ASCENDING THE GRADE TO SHAHGAI

Previous page and this page: Scenes along the Khyber Pass line.

The Berlin-Tegel firm of August Borsig was once one of Germany's biggest locomotive builders. A modest number by the company's standards, in 1930–31 Borsig delivered sixty narrow and broad gauge steam locomotives, steam boilers and tenders for India. Ten new tenders (Borsig Nos 4626–4635) were ordered in 1931 for the NWR, to be hauled by XC class locomotives Nos 1858–1867.

Pakistan Western Railway SGC class 0-6-0 locomotive No. 1260 heads a freight train in 1970. This old-timer was built by the North British Locomotive Company under the works number 20034 of 1912.

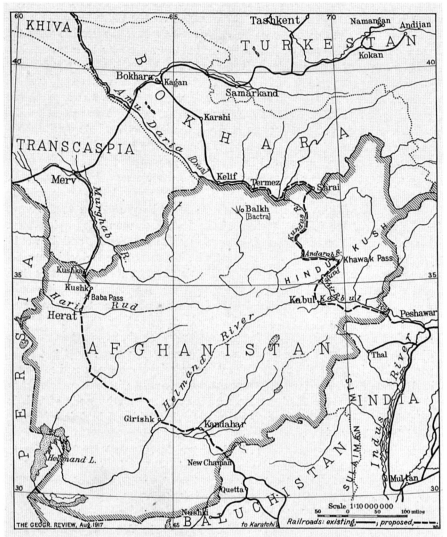

FIG. 2—Outline map showing in greater detail the proposed connections between the Russian and the Indian railway systems through Afghanistan. Scale, 1:10,000,000.

Large-scale plans to link India with the rest of Asia and Europe existed long before the First World War. This map is an example of one such plan. Standard, Russian and Indian gauges would have come together in Afghanistan. In reality, due to the nature of the country (geographical and political) this kind of hub was never created.

During the Cold War, India remained neutral and although it was never inclined towards communism, Russia was considered as a possible ally. A Trans-Himalayan Railway was proposed to connect the Soviet Union with India. Starting from Frunze (now Bishkek, the capital of Kyrgyzstan), the line would have crossed into China. At Kashi, it would have connected with Urumqi. The Karakoroum would have been crossed west of Mount K2 and the line would continue via Gilgit and Srinagar to Jammu, now the terminus of Indian Railways. In the Soviet Union, however, no project of such a large scale is known to have ever existed and nothing came out of the plan.

LONDON TO BOMBAY IN A WEEK: THE PROPOSED £21,000,000 RAILWAY.

DRAWN BY W. H. ROBINSON.

LINKING UP RUSSIA AND INDIA: THE SUGGESTED INTERNATIONAL LINE THROUGH PERSIA, CONNECTING THE RAILWAYS OF RUSSIA AND INDIA.

The proposed Britain to India railway is another example of ambitious colonial-era dreams. It was a mammoth undertaking in a politically unstable area. This 1910 version of the suggested line would have taken eight days to cover a total distance of 5,554 miles from London to Bombay, via Berlin, Rostov, Baku and Baluchistan, in the process bypassing Afghanistan, all for the price of £40.

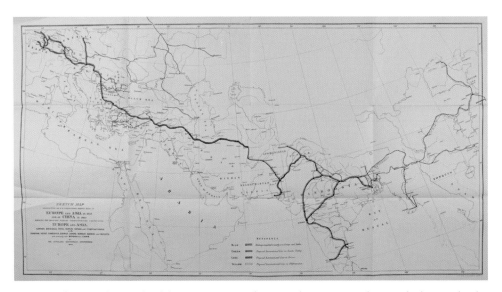

A magnificent plan to build a Britain to China railway was advanced alongside the proposed London to Bombay route. This amazing map from 1882 shows the completed and proposed railways in Europe and Asia, with lines coloured for reference. The route chosen for the awesome London to Changhai line would have taken the passengers across Vienna and Constantinople to Teheran, Kandahar, and Lahore, and from Calcutta to Beijing and the Far East. (QDL collection)

NWR locomotive No. 332 was one of two Armstrong Whitworth 1,300 hp diesel-electric locomotives which were tested in India. It is here seen departing Lahore station in 1935. The two locomotives were intended for the Lahore–Karachi mail service, but one failed already during the preliminary trials. It was then decided to recondition both locomotives. The tests ended when the diesel engines, generators, and traction motors were sent back to England.

Considered as the most famous NWR photo, this iconic view shows XA class 4-6-2 locomotive No. 266x (Vulcan Foundry, 1929) heading a passenger train over the Louise Margaret Bridge, in the Chappar Rift.

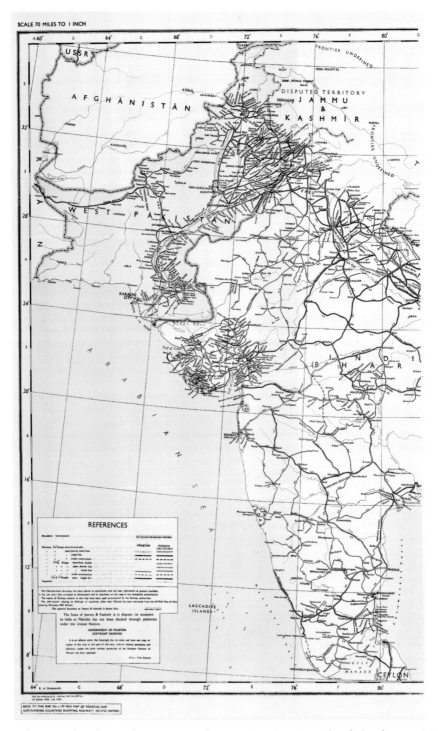

The railways of India and Western Pakistan in 1956. Much of the former NWR system (marked in blue) remained across the border, now out of reach from Delhi and elsewhere in India.

The Bolan Pass line in February 1997. Pakistan Railways ARPW20 type diesel locomotive No. 3830 was built by ALCO in 1957. Here it is seen shortly after leaving Dozan station. Note the catch siding to the left, designed to stop runaway trains in the 1 in 25 grade through the Dozan Gorge. (Alexandre Gilliéron)

Between Sibi and Quetta, a cloud of black smoke towers over PR diesel locomotive No. 3830 as it struggles to bring a passenger train up the Bolan Pass to the summit at Kolpur in February 1997. (Alexandre Gilliéron)

Vulcan Foundry-built PR (ex-NWR) HGS class locomotive No. 2277 heads a Steam Safari special train through the Bolan Pass in February 1997. (Alexandre Gilliéron)

PR (ex-NWR) SGS class locomotive No. 2471 was built by Vulcan Foundry in 1920. Nearly eighty years later, in February 1997, it was captured on film on departure from Attock City to Peshawar with a passenger train. Dating back to the same period as the locomotive in this photo, semaphores are used in Pakistan to this day. (Alexandre Gilliéron)

PR (ex-NWR) SGS class locomotive No. 2471 with a mixed train on the Taxila–Havelian (north-west of Rawalpindi) branch line in February 1997. (Alexandre Gilliéron)

In 1982, it was still possible to take the Friday-only train from Peshawar to Landi Kotal, near the Afghan border. Several switchbacks were built along this spectacular line. This photo shows the first reversing station at Medanak, seen from the considerable height of the next reversing station at Shahgai. With one PR (ex-NWR) 0-6-0 attached to one end of the train, a second locomotive is visible at the other end. Compare the armed guard in this photo with the one illustrated on page 25. (Paul Graalman)

In the far north of Pakistan, the 762 mm gauge Kohat–Thal line was once a British frontier railway close to the border with Afghanistan. The two other 762 mm lines in this remote part of British-ruled India connected Mari Indus with Bannu, with its branch to Tank, and the Bostan to Zhob line. In 1983, ZB class locomotive No. 206, a 2-6-2 built by Hannoversche Maschinenbau AG (Hanomag) in 1932, is taking water somewhere along the line. A decade later, by 1992, it was reported that Kohat–Thal line had been closed.

As was often the case elsewhere in British-ruled India, Langar station was built as a small fort near Jand, in Attock District (Punjab). Seventy years after the Partition of India in 1947, the station still retains its colonial-era charm. (Omar Mukhtar Khan)

Bird's-eye view of Attock Bridge, in a photo taken by RAF photographer Sgt William Devon. This bridge carries the main line from Rawalpindi to Peshawar across the Indus River. It consisted of three land spans and two channel spans. These were supported on steel trestles, the central support rising to a height of 120 feet from a small island in the middle of the river. The steel trestle piers were later encased in concrete and widened. The two channel spans were replaced by stronger cantilever ones. Attock was formerly known as Campbellpur, after Field Marshal Colin Campbell, 1st Baron Clyde (20 October 1792–14 August 1863).

The Lansdowne Bridge spans the Indus River between the cities of Sukkur and Rohri, on the Lahore–Karachi main line in the Sindh province of Pakistan. When completed in 1889, it was the longest rigid girder bridge in the world. This breathtaking bridge was named after Lord Lansdowne, Viceroy of India, and was another of Sir Alexander Meadows Rendel's outstanding engineering achievements in India. It has since then been replaced with Ayub Bridge, which was inaugurated in May 1962 as the first railway bridge in the world to be slung on coiled wire rope suspenders.

South-east of Quetta, Mach station is located midway between Spezand and Sibi. On 3 May 2001, ALCO-built PR diesel locomotive No. 3842 leaves Mach with the Chiltan Express for Lahore. It will now continue descending the 4 per cent grade Bolan Pass. In November 2015, a serious accident occurred on this section when the Rawalpindi-bound Jaffar Express was derailed only a few kilometers from Mach after the brakes failed as the train sped downhill. (Phil Cotterill)

PR diesel locomotive No. 3825 leaves Quetta with the 11.30 to Rawalpindi. (Phil Cotterill)

Nine EMD-powered diesels (model ML3) were built in Australia for Pakistan in 1955 by Clyde Engineering of Granville, New South Wales. Photos of them in action are few and far between. PR No. 2105 was captured on shed at Padidan (on the main line between Kotri and Rohri Junction) on 4 February 1976, in the company of ex-NWR steam veterans. There have been no sightings of the Clyde diesels for many years and the general consensus is that they have all been scrapped. (Mark Carter collection)

PR (ex-NWR) HGS class locomotive No. 2295 (Vulcan Foundry No. 3671 of 1923) at Karachi station in 1960. Of the 133 2-8-0s of this class which ended up in Pakistan in 1947 (NWR Nos 2178–2310), only a handful escaped the cutter's torch.

Painted in dark green, ex-NWR passenger coach 826 carries the official Pakistan Railways inscription in this photo from 1960. Curiously, the title in Arabic reads 'Pakistan Railway', presumably thanks to British influence in that part of the world.

The Patiala State Monorail Trainway (PSMT) was wholly independent from the North Western Railway. It is, however, mentioned here for two reasons. Originally located in Patiala, in south-eastern Punjab, this one of its kind, single-track railway is known to have served the NWR station by the same name. Secondly, the PSMT is a small passenger steam train which, oddly enough, is capable of travelling on only one rail, with balance maintained by large supporting road wheels. It was in fact India's second such monorail system, after the Kundala Valley Railway, which was built in the south of India and was eventually converted to an ordinary railway in 1908. The PSMT owned four 0-3-0 steam locomotives, built by the Berlin firm of Orenstein & Koppel in 1907. Its locomotives were equipped with three double-flanged driving wheels, which were mounted on the centre of each of the three axles. The PSMT was operational until 1927. Post-closure, one of its four steam locomotives was saved and restored at the railway workshops at Amritsar. Nowadays it is preserved at the Indian National Railway Museum in New Delhi.

Located in the vicinity of Islamanad, Golra Sharif is Pakistan's equivalent of a national railway museum where NWR relics and memorabilia may be viewed. The museum, which was opened in October 2003, takes great pride in a small collection of vintage locomotives and rolling stock, exhibited in a nearby yard. On display are steam and electric locomotives, a postal van, a saloon car used by the last Indian viceroy, Lord Mountbatten, and another saloon car previously belonging to the Maharaja of Jodhpur.

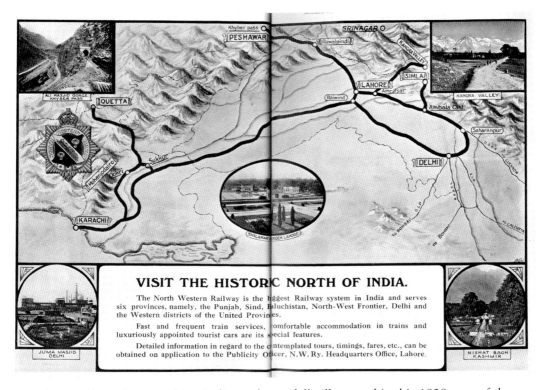

VISIT THE HISTORIC NORTH OF INDIA.

The North Western Railway is the biggest Railway system in India and serves six provinces, namely, the Punjab, Sind, Baluchistan, North-West Frontier, Delhi and the Western districts of the United Provinces.

Fast and frequent train services, comfortable accommodation in trains and luxuriously appointed tourist cars are its special features.

Detailed information in regard to the contemplated tours, timings, fares, etc., can be obtained on application to the Publicity Officer, N.W. Ry. Headquarters Office, Lahore.

The wonders of pre-partition India are beautifully illustrated in this 1929 map of the North Western Railway. The attractions in this huge part of the country were many, such as Shalamar Garden in Lahore and the amazing scenery of Kashmir and Punjab. Direct connections to Bombay and Calcutta were provided from Delhi.

THE NORTH-WESTERN STATE RAILWAY, INDIA.—BRIDGE OVER THE INDUS AT SUKKUR PASS.

The elegant and stylish Sukkur Pass Railway Bridge. This three-span bridge carried the North Western State Railway over the Indus River at Sukkur, where it was divided into two channels. The channel crossed by the bridge was known as the Sukkur Pass, while the Lansdowne Bridge crossed the Rori Channel. The whole of the superstructure of these bridges was constructed by Westwood, Baillie & Co. in Britain before being sent to India.

The Trans-Baluchistan (Quetta–Zahidan) Railway was a British military route between India and Persia (now Iran). It became known as the 'Nushki Extension' as well as the 'Lonely Line', covering hundreds of miles through the barren and empty wasteland. This photo shows Hubert Waters, standing at the far left, a civil engineer who was sent to assist a group of British sappers and miners in the construction of a railway to the Persian border around 1918. For his service on the railways and on the North-West Frontier in 1918–19, he was awarded the Afghan War Medal. (Wikipedia)

From an album of photos taken by a 9th British Middlesex Regiment soldier during the First World War in Mesopotamia and India comes this fascinating view of a British military train on the way from Nowshera to Rawalpindi (Punjab). Note the fixed bayonets.

From the same album as the previous photo, this picture shows different types of NWR passenger cars forming a British military train in Punjab, a century ago.

An undated photo of a construction train at Landi Kotal. Only 5 km away from the Afghan border, Landi Kotal was the terminus of the Khyber Pass Railway and, at 1,072 m, the highest station on that military line.

The front page of the program of the official opening of the Khyber Pass Railway, held at Jamrud on 2 November 1925. The event was covered by the press, with the following extract from the 3 November 1925 issue of *The Times*: 'In brilliant sunshine and in the presence of distinguished assembly, Sir Charles Innes, the Railway Member of the Governor General's Council, acting on behalf of the Viceroy, today performed the ceremony of opening the Khyber Railway. After a speech in which Sir Clement Hindley, Chief Commissioner of Railways, praised the marvelous achievement of the engineers, especially Colonel Hearn and Mr. Victor Bayley, and the cooperation of political and military officers, Sir Charles Innes, amid cheers, pulled the lever which released the gates and threw open the line leading through the grim Pass to the Afghan border. He declared that he believed the railway would stir men's imagination far beyond the limits of British India, and would bring profit to people who had hitherto existed with difficulty on meagre livelihood from the land. The Political Agent and twenty Afridi Maliks were presented to Sir Innes, the Maliks adding a picturesque touch to a remarkable scene. The guests then left for Landi Kotal in special trains, the line rising by loops and spirals, over high bridges, through thirty four tunnels and several gorges. The journey created unbounded admiration in the minds of all at the manner in which the difficulties had been surmounted by the engineers.'

Halfway between Sibi and Quetta, this photo shows a passenger train pulling out of Mach station. Completely surrounded by the dry desert, Mach station also included a shed and a turntable. The photo highlights the station building's beautiful architecture. (ETH Zurich)

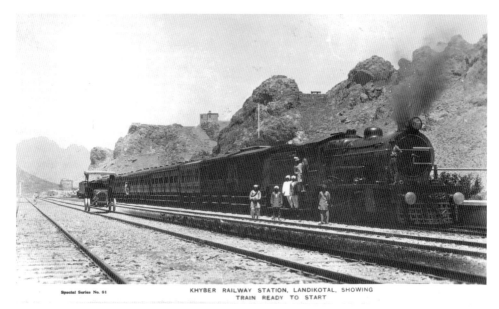

NWR Class HGS 2-8-0 steam locomotive No. 2252 is ready to start out of Landi Kotal station with a passenger train in a vintage postcard. No. 2252 was delivered new by Kitson Locomotive Works of Leeds as works number 5278 of 1920. Note the small railcar occupying the adjacent track.

From a collection of photos taken by a soldier of the Royal Sussex Regiment, this photo shows two NWR 2-8-0 steam locomotives double heading a train in the Khyber Pass, up the steep climb to Landi Kotal in 1929.

Official works photo of NWR 0-4-0T steam locomotive 2 (William Bagnall Locomotive Works, Stafford, 2585 of 1938). This tiny locomotive was placed in service at the railway's Dhilwan Creosoting Plant.

RAILWAY OUTRAGE IN INDIA
The night mail train running between Delhi and Simla, which was deliberately derailed a few miles beyond Ambala on April 6. Many Government officials were travelling in the train.

Above and below: Two notable examples of accidents and incidents on the North Western Railway. In the first photo, dated to 6 April 1931, the Delhi–Simla night mail train was deliberately derailed a few miles beyond Ambala station. Many government officials were travelling in the train. A far worse fate befell the unfortunate passengers of the NWR train in the second photo. In a violent head on collision in Montgomery (now called Sahiwal in Pakistan) on 19 August 1924, 107 passengers were killed and 104 were injured.

INDIAN RAILWAY DISASTER.
The locomotives of two passenger trains came into collision at Montgomery, near Lahore, 107 persons being killed and 104 injured. An assistant station-master was arrested later on a charge of criminal negligence.

The wagon in this photo has a wooden construction and block buffers, with a single brake block. It was built by the Caledonian Railway to St Rollox Works diagram 19 in 1884. On the wagon is a new North Western Railway steam locomotive boiler, bound for Karachi. The photo was probably taken in Glasgow in 1903 at the Heinrich Dübs siding. In the same year, Dübs merged with two other locomotive manufacturers to create the giant North British Locomotive Company.

NWR Class WL 4-6-2 locomotive 102 standing at Lahore on 11 November 1948 (Vulcan Foundry 4780 of 1939), being prepared for trials. On an earlier trial with this class, a maximum speed of 72 mph was reached. The speed record was described as 'fairly creditable performance with driving wheels of 5' 7" diameter'.

Above and below: The Silver Arrow was a short-lived streamlined passenger train operated by Indian Government Railways in 1947. Regarded as a 'train of the future', the locomotive assigned to the haul the Silver Arrow was NWR Class WL No. 103, sister locomotive of 102 in the previous photo. It carried the nameplate *NEW INDIA* and was sheathed in a streamlined aluminum casing with a red band.

The North Western Railway of India coat of arms. Following the Partition of India and the creation of Pakistan, the railway's title was accordingly changed to Pakistan Western Railway on the Pakistani side of the border with India. It now goes by the name of Pakistan Railways.

Model of 2-8-2 locomotive built by the Canadian War Department for the North Western State Railway of India, made in the railway workshops at Lahore, and exhibited at the Indian Railway Post-War Exhibition held at New Delhi from March 24-31, 1946

A charming scale model of a 2-8-2 locomotive built in Canada for the North Western Railway. This fine model was made in the railway workshops at Lahore and proudly displayed at the Indian Railways Postwar Exhibition in New Delhi in March 1946.

Equally inspiring is this model of HGS class locomotive No. 2216, on display at Attock station. (Wikipedia)

Little imagination is needed to appreciate the enormous effort that was needed to build the various railway lines throughout the North Western Province. One of many outstanding examples of the superb engineering skills demonstrated in the construction of the line to Quetta is shown in this photo of Elgin Bridge, in the Dozan range of the Bolan Pass. (Salman Rashid)

Panoramic view of Attock Khurd station – perhaps the most picturesque railway station in all of Pakistan. Lovingly described as a little doll's house of a building with a pitched red roof and sitting under the crenulated turrets of the magnificent Attock Bridge, it belongs in a film set. (Salman Rashid)

Canadian-built Pakistan Railways 2-8-2 Class CWD locomotive No. 5157 and passenger train at Khanewal in 1988. The locomotive's tender deserves a close look, having been decorated with a pair of flags between the railway company's initials.

Old meets new. Pakistan Railways diesel locomotive No. 3748 (Alco, 1962) hauls a passenger train at Multan station in 1980. Ex-NWR Class XA1 4-6-2 locomotive No. 2686 (Vulcan Foundry, 1931) is partly visible to the right. 113 locomotives of this class were built by Vulcan Foundry in 1929–31 and 1935. Upon partition in 1947, thirty-seven went to Pakistan; the other seventy-six remained in India.

Howard Fogg painting from the Alco Products, Inc. collection

ALCO *1950/1800 hp "World" locomotive in Kotri station. The 125 ALCO diesel-electrics on Pakistan's North Western Railway operate one million miles per month.*

Official Alco Locomotive Works color drawing of Pakistan Railways diesel locomotive No. 2042. Designated ALPW18, forty-eight units of this type were delivered to Pakistan in 1958.

Pakistan Railways diesel No. 4019 approaches Rohri Junction with the Sind Express from Quetta in 1988. The locomotive was built by GE in Erie in 1971. The trackside sign, halfway down the train reads, 'Engines to whistle throughout the cuttings.' (Phil Cotterill)

LINKE-HOFMANN-BUSCH

WAGGON · FAHRZEUG · MASCHINEN GMBH

Dieselhydraulischer Triebwagen mit Beiwagen
für die North Western Railway von Pakistan

Baujahr 1958

In addition to diesel locomotives, in 1958 Pakistan Railways took delivery of a few German-made diesel hydraulic railcars built by Linke Hofmann Busch. This official LHB works photo provides a clear view of one of the new railcars.

25 KV ac electric locomotive No. 7028 departs Lahore for Khanewal in 1988. Thirty
units of this class (BCU30E) were built in Britain in 1967. All are reported as having
been taken out of service due to theft of the wires. (Phil Cotterill)

Oil-fired BESA (British Engineering Standards Association) Class SGS (Standard
Goods, Superheated) 0-6-0 locomotive No. 2448 (Vulcan Foundry, 1920) at Kotri
Junction shed on 18 December 1993. Behind it are HGS 2-8-0 No. 2237 (Kitson,
1919–20) and a steam crane. (Nigel Tout)

BESA 'Standard Goods' class SGC 0-6-0 locomotive 1225 (Vulcan Foundry 1911-2) at Kotri Junction shed on 18 December 1993. SGC class locomotives were originally built with saturated boilers but were later converted with superheated boilers, giving them the distinctive elbowed steam pipes. (Nigel Tout)

Metre gauge, oil-fired BESA Class SP 4-6-0 No. 140 (Kerr Stuart, 1921) under repair early on the cold morning of 19 December 1993 at Mirpur Khas locomotive shed, east of Karachi. (Nigel Tout)

Metre gauge Class YD 2-8-2 729 (Nippon of Japan, 1952–53) departs from Mirpur Khas station on 19 December 1993 with a local train taking the clockwise route around the metre gauge loop through the villages south of Mirpur Khas. (Nigel Tout)

Metre gauge BESA Class SP 4-6-0 No. 138 (Kerr Stuart, 1921) on departure from Jhudo with a train heading back to Mirpur Khas on 19 December 1993. Note the beautifully decorated blue truck to the left. (Nigel Tout)

Broad gauge, oil-fired Class CWD 2-8-2 locomotives at Samasata locomotive shed on 20 December 1993. On the right, No. 5690 was built by Montreal Locomotive Works, Canada, in 1945. Here it is under maintenance with the driving wheels removed, revealing the bar frames typical of North American practice. On the left is No. 5170, built by the Canadian Locomotive Company, also in 1945. (Nigel Tout)

Class SGS 0-6-0 2465 (Vulcan Foundry, 1920) crosses a dried-up river near Khewra, north-west of Lahore, with a train from Malakwal on 21 December 1993. (Nigel Tout)

Dramatic view of Class SGS 0-6-0 No. 2470 (Vulcan Foundry, 1920) with a late afternoon passenger train between Lilla and Malakwal on 22 December 1993. (Nigel Tout)

The Khyber Pass Railway was built for strategic reasons to reach the border with Afghanistan. It rises 2,000 feet in 21 miles, requiring a locomotive on each end of the train. Class HGS 2-8-0 steam locomotives power a passenger train through a tunnel up the Khyber Pass on 23 December 1993. (Nigel Tout)